NETWORKING AND COLLABORATION

AN ENTREPRENEUR'S GUIDE TO OVERCOMING THE
FEAR OF NETWORKING AND MASTERING
THE ART OF COLLABORATION

Copyright © 2016

All rights reserved. No part of this book may be reproduced, stored in a retrieval system, or transmitted in any form or by any means, electronic, mechanical, photocopying, recording, scanning, or otherwise, without the prior written permission of the publisher.

Disclaimer

All the material contained in this book is provided for educational and informational purposes only. No responsibility can be taken for any results or outcomes resulting from the use of this material.

While every attempt has been made to provide information that is both accurate and effective, the author does not assume any responsibility for the accuracy or use/misuse of this information.

Table of Contents

INTRODUCTION ……………………………………………1

CHAPTER 1 : PREPARING FOR THE OPPORTUNITY……5

CHAPTER 2 : IT'S ALL IN THE FOLLOW-UP……………..8

CHAPTER 3 : THE ART OF COLLABORATION …………12

   REASONS WHY YOU SHOULD CONSIDER COLLABORATION AS AN ENTREPRENEUR:………..16

   7 TIPS FOR SUCCESSFUL BUSINESS NETWORKING…………………………………………..19

ABOUT THE AUTHOR…………………………………….24

INTRODUCTION

Collaboration is a powerful tool for all entrepreneurs irrespective of your industry, you'll find "Big Businesses" secure the art of collaboration as a mode of marketing. Forming those connections not only helps to grow your business, but it also provides you with the opportunity to create influence to a different group of potential clients and/or collaborative partners.

The biggest challenge for most new brands is lack of awareness, which is why more than 80% of businesses have identified acquisition of new customers "finding new customers" as one of their biggest challenges. Social Media can have a phenomenal impact on your business if used the correct way. However, social media is not the end-all-be-all of marketing, I am a strong believer that collaboration remains one of the best ways to increase your influence and strengthen your marketing plan.

Business networking is the exchange of information or services among individuals, groups, or institutions; *specifically* the cultivation of productive relationships for employment or business. Networking has a lot to do with connection between a set of entities whose goal is to form lasting relationships that are mutually beneficial. Properly increasing your network has an uncanny ability to cultivate an increase in your net-worth. Essentially, networking involves an entrepreneur making connections with the right set of people in order to expand his or her business. In more definitive terms, it is an effective marketing method for creating and taking advantage of sales opportunities. The amazing thing about networking is the fact that it can come at a very low cost to entrepreneurs. It requires setting aside strategic time, and making connections through referrals, introductions, meetings, gatherings or via electronic means such as email, phone, social media, etc.

In business, you always hear that "No man is an island" and "You can't run a multi-billion dollar business alone." These statements really have some validity because the network of people you have surrounding you determines how far you'll go in life, as well as in business. Networking allows you to expand your vision to limitless opportunities that would normally be obscure, connecting your innovativeness to the likeness of another. Not only is it important to develop sound marketing strategy using ad, social media, and the likes, understanding and employing the tools of networking and collaboration should be a major part of your marketing plan.

Most of the time when we're coaching, and we ask our clients about their current marketing strategy, they tend to provide us with their social media statistic, advertisement on the TV and billboards, and referrals, it's very rare that entrepreneurs include networking as a part of their marketing plan. I've found that connecting with someone face to face and not only sharing your products and services with them but also sharing your story with them allows them to form a connection with both what you do and why you do it, evoking the response for them to share it with others, which will inadvertently help to increase your level of influence which can then increase your sales in a positive way.

One major underlying problem that we've found amongst some of the boldest entrepreneurs we've met has been their FEAR of networking. You'd be surprised at how many entrepreneurs loath the networking experience. They'd rather be behind the computer kicking out content and creating book, heck I was one of them. I hated talking about myself, trying to formulate the right words to grab their attention, how to peg if they are truly interested, and most importantly how to overcome those awkward silent moments. Networking for me always felt like I walked into the room with my own personal spotlight. The problem was that I had no control over it. In business, we're always taught that if you find a need then as an entrepreneur your job should be to solve the problem. I have the tendency to be very analytical at times. I had to find the need and address the problem within my own organization.

Keystone Business Institute- Simple needs analysis

The need = engaging and building new business relationships

The resolve = Networking

The problem = ME

The strategic solution- events, collaborations

Within the pages of this book, we will tackle this issue with implementable action steps.

CHAPTER 1

PREPARING FOR THE OPPORTUNITY

When you have the opportunity to network, whether you are in a structured networking environment or random impromptu, remember to never set your mind on what your new contact can do for you. Always engage with the helping mindset.

You can do this by asking them this very simple question:

"How can I help you?"

Asking this question changes the receiver's mindset from this is a person who's providing a sells pitch to this is an individual who wants to build a relationship. Your ultimate goal when it comes to networking should be to build lasting relationships. Build with honesty, build with integrity, and build authentically. Being honest with who you are and what you do and where you are right now! You never know what resources and tools the other person has that could help push your business to the next level.

Building of relationships with other entrepreneurs takes time, which means it is a continuous process that over time will yield long term results. When preparing for the opportunity, keep in mind that business networking isn't necessarily about making direct sales on the spot, though sometimes that most definitely may occur; rather it is more about the professional connections that you're able to make, gaining trust, and sharing new opportunities for business expansion.

As an entrepreneur, you cannot afford to shy away from business gatherings, meetings or the chance to meet people. Listen, we know it's not easy speaking in public. However, with the right support, preparation, and practice, there is no way around it, you will have to "get out;" leave your comfort zone and try new things.

When you have an opportunity to share your business with someone else, your goal should be to share enough information that would cause them to be intrigued by what you do. Show them the true need for your services along with why you do what you do. Encourage them to continue to engage with you and your brand.

Here are some quick tips to think about when tailoring your overall message:

1. Explain what you do in a clear fashion. (The person on the receiving end should not have to ask questions to gain clarity on the overall description of your business.)

2. Explain how and why you do what you do (At what moment did you say "Yes" to your business?)

3. Create a visual that allows the receiver to see themselves in your vision as either a collaborator or a customer.

Remember: Even if you don't form a business collaboration with the receiver, you still have the opportunity to gain a new client. Here at Keystone Business Institute, we call this the no man left behind theory.

At the end of the day, a good entrepreneur knows how to pitch their story. A great entrepreneur knows how to pitch their story in a fashion that yields results. Be your authentic self, we can tell when you're being phony; there is a vast difference between being nervous and being phony. When you are unapologetically yourself, you won't have to remember what identity you portrayed to others. We want the real you; we have to be ok with the fact that some will love us and some won't; either way that's ok!

CHAPTER 2

IT'S ALL IN THE FOLLOW-UP

The hard part is over; you did it, you attended the event, you connected and received contact and follow-ups. Now comes the point where many networkers fail to follow through after initiating a conversation with someone, it's the follow-up. If you are a master procrastinator, here is where you'll have to push through the dreadful spirit of procrastination, and there are many books written on the topic of overcoming procrastination, we suggest you conduct a Google search and find the book that best fits your needs. Deal with the reasons why you procrastinate and provide opportunities for yourself to overcome them. Procrastination has been a silent killer of many small businesses. You can't afford to procrastinate, and when I say afford, I mean literally!

Immediately following the event, take a moment and prioritize your connections, connect with those you feel you made the strongest connection with first, make sure you're making small reminder notes for yourself during the event. Your initial follow-up should take place within 24 hours of acquiring these new contacts. Below are several tips to help you conduct your follow ups:

1. **Send a quick (follow-up) email-** This quick email should be short, sweet, and to the point. You have 'broken the ice' by meeting them at the networking event. The next thing to do is 'melt the ice' which can be achieved by sending a simple email to them; be sure to reference the event that brought you together initially. Then don't forget to add some type of invitation to meet within the week. This email shouldn't be anything long or complex, it should show your interest in connecting with the person.

2. **Connect on LinkedIn-** As an entrepreneur, in today's times, you are expected to have a LinkedIn profile. Your LinkedIn profile is regarded as your professional social media profile compared to your other social media profiles such as Facebook, Twitter, Instagram, etc. Furthermore, LinkedIn has a variety of tools that will assist you with keeping your contact at the forefront of your mind.

3. **Create 'reconnect files'-** These are monthly reminders that can be designed within an excel sheet, that help you to stay in touch with all the contacts made, which will allow you to keep your contacts organized. Usually, these sheets are color-coded to differentiate each set of contacts and should contain

some information about how you met and what you've discussed with the person or group of persons. Set your alerts to check your reconnect file. When you reach out to your connection, set up another meeting or send some important information; like an invitation to an upcoming event or a very useful article.

4. **Show them that you care-** This is a straightforward concept, it just involves finding ways and opportunities to show your connections that you're not just doing business with them you genuinely want to do life with them as well. Remembering their birthday and other special occasions of your contacts by simply sending heartfelt wishes to them, sending a thank you card, etc.

5. **Set up a meeting in person-** Now, this is your chance to cement your relationship with your client further and as a result, the objective of the meeting has to be clearly stated so that both parties can prepare accordingly in order to achieve maximum excellent results. The place to meet should be easily accessible with good parking space and some tranquility that will really provide enough space to talk without any distraction (noise). The key is to allow them to ask most of the questions and then answer them with plans or necessary information about your business. Go into this meeting with the mindset of how can I serve you?

6. **A network of 1,000-** You never know who they know, any contact with whom you reach out to and relate with most likely knows hundreds, if not thousands of other people who can be potential clients and/or collaborators. This idea alone makes the power of your conversation exponential. It is therefore important to understand that when you're talking to someone, you're actually speaking to their entire network. The same goes for them with you. The most effective form of marketing through word of mouth is activated when someone says, "I know someone who can do that," and that someone should be you!

CHAPTER 3

THE ART OF COLLABORATION

Collaboration is a powerful tool for all entrepreneurs irrespective of your industry, you'll find "Big Businesses" secure the art of collaboration as a mode of marketing. Forming those connections not only helps to grow your business, but it also provides you with the opportunity to create influence to a different group of potential clients and/or collaborative partners.

The biggest challenge for most new brands is lack of awareness — which is why more than 80% of businesses have identified acquisition of new customers "finding new customers" as one of their biggest challenges. Social Media can have a phenomenal impact on your business if handled the correct way. However, social media is not the end-all-be-all of marketing, I am a strong believer that collaboration remains one of the best ways to increase your influence and strengthen your marketing plan.

Here are 5 tips that I've found that will help you with your ability to sustain successfully collaborations.

1. **Effective Strategy-** All effective marketing strategy starts with a clear idea of what you want to achieve, essentially

what results you would like to see, but be realistic and be set clear expectations, once you are clear about your idea, you can then create collaborative marketing strategies around the idea. Once you understand the concept and why, you can then determine to review your list of potentials and determine which business(s) could also benefit from this idea. Some ideas come directly from the networking experience, don't negate those impromptu collaborative ideas session. However, it's utterly important that your objectives for collaboration must be clearly stated so that the activities you engage in will bring forth your desired results.

2. **Stay true to your brand-** When selecting the business(es) that you may possibly want to collaborate with, you want to select a business that fits your brand and/or has the capability to shift your brand's presence. There is absolutely nothing wrong with asking if there is an alignment of goals, beliefs, and end results with those you wish to collaborate with. Will this collaboration be your current present initiative or will you continue with your normal day to day actions while preparing for the collaboration? You don't want a collaborative initiative to be a detriment to your own business. You have to take the time to ask yourself the hard questions, the opportunity may be good, but are you prepared to truly execute with excellence? We don't want a great opportunity to become a nightmare because we aren't honest with ourselves and the state of our businesses when the

opportunity arises.

3. **Put yourself in your customer's shoes-** Ask questions such as, will this benefit my current clientele, and will this generate new leads? These are some of the questions that you must ask. As a business coach, my job is to create opportunities for our clients, while we position ourselves to generate new leads. Benefits not only to yourself but also your customers should be at the forefront of any marketing activity or collaborative initiative. In order to make an informed decision, you should study and know your customers, their current needs, and wants.

4. **Cash is King… Or maybe not-** A big mistake that a lot of entrepreneurs make is the belief that they need a substantial amount of finances to expand their business or probably go for paid-for sponsorship deals, but it's best to build relationships based on mutual benefit rather than cash exchanges. Once you have already carried out your networking and identified who you want to reach and what you want to achieve, then just examine your 'arsenal' to determine what you have that is of value, which you can offer potential business partners. You could give away products in return for free advertising, offer up competition prizes for editorial coverage, feature other peoples' competitions in your marketing in exchange for featuring in theirs, create an initiative around a mutually supported

topic— the opportunities are endless. Don't get caught up in the *I have nothing to offer mindset*. You are equipped with some valuable content and knowledge, don't negate that because you're small or don't do much marketing. Just take a good look at your business, and you will find what you need to offer to get the right partners.

5. **Focus on the relationship for excellent results**- In return for reaching new customers and promoting your business for little or no cost, be prepared to invest time in creating a strong relationship with your business partner(s). Don't try to 'outsmart' your business partners, but rather be open and honest about what you and your business partner(s) want to achieve, and agree on your common objectives ahead of time. If you get the right balance, you will both want to repeat the activities again and again, which really pays back on the time spent finding, meeting, and working together, setting clear to-dos for all parties involved. Be flexible and creative early in the planning stage. Once you have a central idea for working together, look at all parts of your respective businesses and see how and where you can spread your idea across multiple marketing channels. By amplifying the activity across email, print, adverts or social media, you will get better return on investment for the time you are putting in.

REASONS WHY YOU SHOULD CONSIDER COLLABORATION AS AN ENTREPRENEUR:

1. Collaboration can help reduce the cost of operation.

Collaboration reduces the cost of running a business because most times it involves sharing of the workload as well as ideas between the partners and if there's an agreement in place to divide the expenses between (or among) the partners as the case may be, then the individual entrepreneurs will spend less in running their respective businesses. This means there's a higher chance that you will be getting great value for money invested compared to if you alone is bearing the cost.

2. Collaboration proffers solution to problems easily.

There is power in numbers. Sometimes, a collective effort might be what's needed to achieve a particular goal and as an entrepreneur. There is saying, I'm not sure who originated it, but I love the statement, "If You Want To Go Fast, Go Alone. If You Want To Go Far, Go Together," and this exemplifies the power of collaboration in one sentence. Think about it for a few minutes. Whenever we get faced with a problem as an entrepreneur, most of us immediately go to a partner, mentor, or other trusted resource who acts as a sounding board and helps us work through the problem. The harder the problem is to solve, the more we can benefit from getting the input of someone outside of the situation. And when you add new viewpoints and experiences to the mix, the end result will often go beyond what you originally set out to accomplish.

3. Collaboration can be a source of inspiration.

Two heads are better than one they say. As an entrepreneur, you already have a set routine that helps tp keep you focused and ensure your view of sound operation methods that increase productivity. Focusing only on your way and your routine might make you oblivious to the fact that there might actually be better ways of doing things as well as new tools and techniques that can actually save you money.

While you can read blogs, magazines, and books for inspiration, if you are not sharing and discussing that information with like-minded people, the benefits are limited. This is why collaboration is important as it allows you to get out of your own zone and listen to others while at the same time, it gives you a fresh perspective, triggers your creativity, objectively analyzes incoming information, and updates the data you have so that all can be effectively utilized. Going beyond what you do and see each day to explore collaboration can be inspiring and help you think in a new way.

4. Collaboration helps you grow your network.

Successful entrepreneurs have a common interest in meeting new people and building a list of contacts and colleagues. So, being successful in business requires that you consistently make connections and form alliances because failing to generate new set of customers or clients means that sales will be down and your business will decline. Networking is a must, while it is possible that every contact you make may not result in collaboration; however, every time you reach out to someone to explore the possibility, you are expanding your network.

5. Collaboration is educational.

One of the biggest benefits of collaboration is the opportunity for learning. In fact, every interaction you have with someone outside of your immediate circle can teach you something valuable. Some of the most successful collaborations involve two connoisseurs who bring two very different skill sets, ideas, and strengths to the table. When this happens, education is inevitable; you are most likely to leave the conversation with new ideas and knowledge.

7 TIPS FOR SUCCESSFUL BUSINESS NETWORKING

Having examined what business networking is as well as how to make contacts and also utilize the contacts, let's just run through some tips that an entrepreneur should bear in mind when engaging in business networking. One important thing to consider is that various professional people that are not necessarily within the entrepreneurship or business community can turn out to be very helpful networking contacts such as medical doctors, professors, educators, etc. Therefore, whenever you set out to network for your business, you need to factor in those that are not usually found at business networking events and also those that you come in contact on a daily basis, your doctor, therapists, store managers etc., as they will be very effective in spreading the 'word' about your products and services. As my mother's caregiver, we spent a lot of time waiting for various doctors, so while the nurse was taking my mother's vitals, I was typing away on my computer. He said, "You are always typing, what are you doing?" I shared with him how I was finalizing the release of my first book; he asked me the name and where he could find it. I told him it was on amazon. At our next visit, not only had he ordered it, but he read it and had 10 of his colleagues purchase it as well! Remember, there is power in sharing!

In conclusion, always remember these 7 steps of preparing for a networking opportunity and engaging in a collaborative effort.

1. **Present yourself well-** This starts with your appearance including the way you dress because the way you look will go a long way to determining how serious people will take you even before you say anything. Consequently, you only have a few seconds to make an impression on prospective clients, which means by the time you introduce yourself and talk to them, your words must be succinct and concise so that there is a generation of interest in your business. You need to be able to convey a significant amount of information in a very short time and in few words.

2. **Lend a helping hand-** Ever heard of, "Givers never lack?" It holds true in networking as well. Sometimes, when you're networking, do not be too quick to make it about yourself; try to ask about the interest of the other person and see if you can help. This builds your reputation, and by that your integrity is solidified. People will start talking more about you and will refer others to you; before you know it, clients will start flowing your way and all because you're ready to give to others and lend a helping hand.

3. **Integrity-** It has been said that "A good name is better than a thousand riches," which means no matter what, you must always ensure to keep your integrity. Definitely, nobody is perfect, and mistakes are bound to happen, but then you should be able to accept responsibility for such mistakes and make up for it. Failing to do such might cause some serious damage to your reputation, and you will not want that. So why exactly is integrity important? This is because it is the major ingredient for developing trust without which it will be virtually impossible to engage in business networking and get amazing results.

4. **Focus-** like every endeavor in life wherein success is required, focus is needed particularly in business networking because it's possible to feel there are other means through which clients can be gotten and as a result, not much effort is put into the networking while still expecting excellent results; not going to happen. You need to concentrate efforts on business networking and apply the efforts on a consistent basis in order to get effective results. Also, it is important to be open-minded as opportunities to conduct business or even make new contacts can arise in the least expected places and staying focused is what will allow an entrepreneur to recognize these opportunities and take them.

5. **Explore relevant targets-** This involves checking out the type of networking group you want to join as well as the set of people you want to pitch your business to. Joining a business networking group is great, but you have to be sure it's productive or else it will end up being a waste of time and efforts. So, that means carrying out proper research and study before picking your targets and approaching them. You can use factors like geographical location, size, sector, trade, and organized networking groups to determine your targets and after clearly 'sizing' them up, you can then make your move.

6. **Follow up-** Always try your best to stay true to your words and follow up on contacts made as that will give people the feeling that you are determined and reliable. This requires your commitment which will still be a fallout of you being focused. Give prospective clients the impression that they can rely and depend on you to deliver the products or services at the right time. This will generate more clients for you because previous ones will just keep referring and recommending you; so, don't forget this tip.

7. **Plan your networking-** An endeavor without a well-defined plan will most likely make no real headway as it will be going in different directions without achieving much. So, for

successful networking, there has to be a plan on how to go about the networking like the amount of time to be spent each week or month to meet new people, time to call, the number of events to be attended per week or per month as the case may be. Basically, your plan should contain a strategy for time management so that you will not be exhausted and then find yourself unable to do other activities. Ensure you know exactly what you want to achieve from the networking so that you will be able to channel your efforts better.

All in all, do not be afraid to take the next big step as that might be just what is separating your business and immense success. Conquer that fear of not being able to meet people or whether they will really want to hear what you have to say. Be confident and believe in yourself and let people see that confidence in you. Definitely, not all businesses you network with will be a good fit for collaboration with your business, but that does not mean you should not try to network at all because failure to might mean some opportunities passing you by. It's time to get out, meet people and expand your business, no more fear. It's time to #MOVEAFRAID!

ABOUT THE AUTHOR

| Entrepreneur | Author | Coach, Mentor | Advocate |
| Speaker | Forex Trading Investor |

Keandra Ward is loved for her unique education and training style along with her pure passion for every aspect helping the people that she serves; operate at their fullest potential by overcoming their excuses and walking boldly towards their destiny. Originally from Cleveland, Ohio; Keandra has worked as a self-employed business owner for over 20 years. She began her career in a salon at the age of 14 and opened her first salon at the age of 18. She holds a B.A. in Psychology from the University of South Florida and a Masters in Internet Marketing from Full Sail University.

Additionally, Keandra currently holds over 40 certifications in all areas of business, cosmetology and makeup artistry. Her experience as a manager, trainer, and quality specialist for a fortune 500 freight logistics company helped her to develop her business management and training skills.

Keandra opened NV beauty Industry Consultants now The B.O.M.B Mentoring Group in 2010 providing business and personal development news, courses and business training for start-ups and businesses looking to up level the internal and external strategies of their brands current design. As a mother of one and as her mothers caregiver, she understands the importance of making her money work for her; as a Forex (Foreign Exchange Trading) investor Keandra teaches her clients and others how to change their financial futures through learning a skillset that teaches them how to multiply their money and become their own investors.

Keandra has worked within her community by giving of her time and talents to various churches, fashion shows, high school cosmetology programs, and organizations.

As a licensed minister, her Love for God, People, Business and Ministry has allowed her to continuously take her message to the masses through her #Moveafraid entrepreneurs network, her book projects and speaking engagements.

A word from Keandra

Don't let you, stop YOU, from succeeding! Activate your faith by overcoming your fears. You're built for this, there's someone out there that needs exactly what you have. It's time for you to SHOW UP!

I would love to stay connected with you

Visit me online at

thebombmentoring.com

and on social media @thebombmentor

www.ingramcontent.com/pod-product-compliance
Lightning Source LLC
Chambersburg PA
CBHW040302220526
45473CB00002B/561